# SUMMER ON SCILLY

This is my third book of sketches of the Isles of Scilly; the first being 'sketches of scilly', followed by 'winter on scilly', the companion book to this one.
I've also published sketchbooks of St Ives, the Fal Estuary & Fowey. My latest assignment has been recording the making of the Eden Project.

Published by Dyllansow Truran, Croft Prince, Mount Hawke, Truro, Cornwall TR48EE
Printed by R. Booth at the Troutbeck Press, Antron Hill, Mabe, Penryn, Cornwall TR109HH
ISBN 1 85022 136 7 (paperback)

waiting for boats . . .

At old Grimsby on Tresco . . . .

April 26th

Yesterday I heard the first cuckoo,
& the first swallow is swooping around
my head right now. Its obviously the day to start my summer diary

More swallows are skimming low along the beach. The sun feels HOT
& first sea pinks are in bud - I can just about believe that winter
is gone!   3

OLD QUAY 8am. tide falling, S.E wind. clear.

11.15 low tide, changing shadows

Blunt tellin    Limpet    cowries    Painted topshell    wentletrap    Purple toph

4

.45 tide rising fast.

3pm. still rising. A gathering of gulls on the end of the quay

The wind dropped this afternoon. very hot
John Webb says that there's a saying...

The East wind is like a kite,
up by day & down by night!

It seems to be true!

Periwinkle    grey tophell    Dog whelk    cockle

5

Holidays are so exhausting . . .

Tamarisk

hemlock leaves

sea spinach

campions + pink oxalis

yarrow leaves

May. Hot & windy

can't go ANY further . . .

6

Landed at old Grimsby, coffee & ethel's sponge at New Grimsby, walked to Cromwell's Castle, Charles' Castle & back to the new inn for lunch. Beachcombing on Farm Beach, walked round the corner — need a rest before going out to Carn N

Just occasionally we pretend we're on holiday too.

sun & clouds changing light

An afternoon off — out painting with Mandy on the rocks at low tide at the end of Great Bay

May - the best time for wild flowers.

Scarlet Pimpernel open. Wild Garlic, Bermuda Buttercup, campions cranesbill, speedwell & the last of the Scillas in amongst the old Daffodil leaves. Ixias making an exotic splash by the hedge

Ixia

scarlet Pimpernel

Bermuda Buttercup

hairy buds & leaves smooth stem

Just like a tiny forget me not

Common vetch

Rosy Garlic

All these flowers in one small meadow...

Two Cuckoos just flew by cuckooing as they went —
somehow I thought they always perched to do that!

Hop Trefoil

Chickweed

Dovesfoot Cranesbill?

Germander Speedwell!

Sorrel

Buttercup

Celandine

English Catchfly — both pink & white

Ribbed Plantain

9

A day off – a rare day off.
A picnic on little Arthur, looking across to Little Gauilly

Behind the shore line a bank of thrift & mayweed
two kinds of docks, nightshade, foxglove seed heads
sea spinach, orache, stonecrop
Bright orange lichen on the rocks – so bright
in the sun that it hurts the eyes.

11

A blowy morning from the beach under the campsite . . .

And the exact opposite · Not a breath of wind, sea like glass, mist rising

13

May/June & The fields change colour.
The pale green of the new bracken almost
hidden by indian Red & ochre sorrel & the
pinks of Ixias & campions, oxalis & foxgloves..

just over
lifesize →

don't know what
this is, but it's
sitting on
my
sketchbook

Whistling Jack

A field crop, rarely sent to
market now, but grows in old
fields & hedgerows in May,
often amongst scarlet poppies.

an impossible colour – first its too blue, Then its too mauve

The last of the bluebells still bright in the edges of the fields

Aeonium – I think that how you spell it...

masses of flowers this year

lots of bees visiting the flowers

Bush Echium
Not so tall as the tree echium, but crouched & a deeper blue.

Sprawling down cliffs & over sand dunes

Hottentot fig

15

waiting for boats. St. Mary's Quay.
the Scillonian just arrived
Sunny, but strong NW wind.

Firethorn, Spirit, Voyager & Sea Horse
all making for the steps. No one
knows quite where to go.

16

4.30 am. sky lightening to the east. Heavy clouds. Cock crowing &
birds singing.
5.40 The sun comes up behind the hill & behind the clouds.

11am    Hot & sunny, all the cloud gone

18

11.30 - I spoke too soon . . . . .

9.30 & the sun touches the top of the hill

a couple of minutes later ~
~ is gone.

19

shell-seekers looking like some kind of wading birds.

watching the divers...

20

Sunny + hot on Par Beach in July.

Its COLD!

21

late morning - mist lifted, blue & bright.
Groups of figures all along the bay, just staring at the
colours & light on the water — —

22

Afternoon - mist rolling back in. Faint sparkles on the water before the sun disappears.. Just two gulls left on the quay.

Boats everywhere — fishing boats-
large & small, sailing boats & trippers. St. Mary's Quay
crammed at lunchtime with the Scillonian the freight launch &
all the off-Island boats waiting for visitors.

24

The Sea King moored quietly at the quay - total change from an hour ago when the Sea Horse arrived with visitors, luggage, boxes of groceries, parcels & packages. In a few minutes everything is sorted & loaded, all the vans & tractors gone & just one man left - watching . . . . . .

25

Old Quay
Theres a strong easterly
blowing so EVERYONE has
found their way down here.
I've never seen it so busy
July 26th

Pink legs, knobbly knees
& an evil glint in his eye
— & standing right next to me...

A pushchair left in
amongst the nets & pots at the
bottom of the path to the beach

26

keith & Jane back from fishing

olive

pink

green

SC

And home, hot & tired & on the Sea King with Frazer & Tony

Sunny days, Fêtes & Garden Parties

A little added planning worry - Fête days
have to suit the tides, so that boats can
get to the right quay at the right time!

29

August 11th

Each time I peer out from under my plastic sheet more of the landscape has disappeared into grey mist & rain . . .

I'm sitting on a wall in the middle of nowhere hunched under my plastic sheet & a man has just tapped on my shoulder, introduced himself as the owner of a boat I painted & put in a book last year. He pointed her out down in Great Bay & then walked off into the rain ! . . .

Just a normal dull August day . . . so far

10 am . Dark clouds to the West  Rain?! . 10.10 Rain. Not the start of People gathering at Top Rock & Flagstaff . . the eclipse ! 10.30 More . rain . .

This is me.

cheeks & brow, flashes & fireworks..

Dark comes like the light
being turned off
- so fast.
such a strange feeling to see the
light dimming so quickly - from
day to dark in just a few seconds

11.05. cloud breaking up a little..
getting darker , I didnt see any stars & the gulls kept on crying....

11.20 its raining again

31

Tuesday August 17th
The Lyonesse Lady arrives full of groceries r building materials.

Tractors are so heavily laden
They can't lift buckrakes off
the ground

All this hidden by Landrovers, r tractors
Just before the launch arrives

The weather isn't always as good as this...

This is more usual...

Everything has to arrive on the launch, so the whole island knows when you have a new bed, or a washing machine or computer, word goes round that the fresh fruit has arrived (or the bread or the papers! Its hard to keep a secret here...

work still goes on in the fields – bulbs have to
be lifted, & polythene put down to bring
on the early flowers. they're still picking
pinks too . .

34

Greenhouses full of grapes & tomatos
geraniums like trees & exotic flowers...

Pink
bougainvillia

Red

Plumbago

grapes

Red & pink
geraniums

echium

35

A Perfect Day ..... one to remember in the winter
when its cold & wet & windy .
The view from a completely deserted Nor Nour
- only our footprints on the beach

On the way home we landed on the
sand bar off little Gavilly. We should have
written PARADISE in the sand so that people
flying in would know where they were . . .

37

waiting for boats...

At Old Grimsby on Tresco.... r the Quay on St Marys.

HARBOURSIDE HOTEL

Mid season
Busy boats,
long queues,
plenty of time to
people-watch...

Home from shopping — on the
freight boat

tomatoes

plants for...

mushrooms

HANDE FARM PRODUCE

Richard & Sue's boat on the beach.
she looks lovely while she's still
but I don't think I'd want to sail'
her back to Penzance.

The tide still dropping - The divers have
just waded in from their boat on one
of the farthest moorings

Groups of people all over the sand

A hot August day
very bright, but the morning fog
is still hanging around low on the
sea & softening the edges of all the
islands.

shrimping

Jinny always knows the        best places!

41

Richard's contented cows in Dry Field — overlooking the Eastern Isles.

nine bantam chicks
just hatched

walking up from old quay
today I saw a wren
perched on a bracken stem
so tiny & light that the bracken
was n'ot bowed down at all
singing in such a loud voice that
he stopped me in my tracks.

Long evenings to wander through the fields . . . .

Seven cows in the Top field

43

I'm really pleased I've got Daph's mum's old piano in the Gallery...

I've not seen you in Winter,
And I know your storms are wild.
But to all your summer strangers
You're a happy smiling child. — with thanks to Jan Laud...

I was sitting in the Gallery working on the opposite page in late September when in walked Dorothy & Olive, Barrie & Rick from the Exeter Age Concern choir, who proceeded to play & sing Jan's song beautifully....

44

# I WANT TO GO BACK TO ST. MARTINS.

summer evening Gallery parties

I want to go back to St. Martins;
With your bright pink & yellow flowers.
I don't want to dream about you,
But spend all my waking hours
In your green & gentle islands.
Paint the sea cerulean blue;
Glistening rocks with tiny diamonds;
And there's nothing I must do.

Its hard to draw Jan - she moves
so fast shes just a blur!

Seals playing in the shallows,
Seagulls squawking in the air.
Small stone houses in the hollows;
Red boats sailing in winds fair.
Fellow man does not disturb your
creamy sands at ebbing tide,
Where the sun is warm & heavy,
The horizon stretches wide. 45

Bell heather

blue butterflies

Middle of July. Heather already turning the
46 hills purple.

Early August. The bracken turning brown
& ochre already. The ling all flowering

A grey September day -
Keith's cottage. The vines on the
wall leafy & overgrown, geraniums
in flower..

Belladonna's in swing &
drying bracken
& blackberries

47

The boats are emptied now. The last few visitors leaving a rough trip to St. Marys ahead.